Best of Bridge

The Family Slow Cooker

225 All-New Recipes

Robert
ROSE

For complete cataloguing information, see page 331.

Disclaimer
The recipes in this book have been carefully tested by our kitchen and our tasters. To the best of our knowledge, they are safe and nutritious for ordinary use and users. For those people with food or other allergies, or who have special food requirements or health issues, please read the suggested contents of each recipe carefully and determine whether or not they may create a problem for you. All recipes are used at the risk of the consumer.

We cannot be responsible for any hazards, loss or damage that may occur as a result of any recipe use.

For those with special needs, allergies, requirements or health problems, in the event of any doubt, please contact your medical adviser prior to the use of any recipe.

Design and production: Kevin Cockburn/PageWave Graphics Inc.
Layout: Alicia McCarthy/PageWave Graphics Inc.
Editor: Sue Sumeraj
Recipe editor: Jennifer MacKenzie
Proofreader: Kelly Jones
Indexer: Gillian Watts
Photographer: Colin Ericson
Associate photographer: Matt Johannsson
Food stylist: Michael Elliott
Prop stylist: Charlene Ericson

Cover image: Slow Cooker Barbecue Brisket (page 188)

The publisher gratefully acknowledges the financial support of our publishing program by the Government of Canada through the Canada Book Fund.

Published by Robert Rose Inc.
120 Eglinton Avenue East, Suite 800, Toronto, Ontario, Canada M4P 1E2
Tel: (416) 322-6552 Fax: (416) 322-6936
www.robertrose.ca

Printed and bound in China

1 2 3 4 5 6 7 8 9 PPLS 24 23 22 21 20 19 18 17 16

CONTENTS

INTRODUCTION

IT'S TIME TO PULL OUT YOUR SLOW COOKER!

WE TALKED TO OUR FRIENDS, FAMILY AND READERS, AND THE GENERAL CONSENSUS WAS THAT LIFE IS GETTING BUSIER, MONEY IS GETTING TIGHTER, AND PEOPLE AREN'T GETTING ANY LESS HUNGRY. HECK, WE FEEL ALL OF THAT TOO (ESPECIALLY THE NEVER GETTING LESS HUNGRY PART), AND ALL OF US HAVE FAMILIES WHO SEEM TO CONTINUALLY REQUIRE FEEDING. FOR MANY, THE SATISFACTION THAT COMES FROM ASSEMBLING A FEW INGREDIENTS EARLY IN THE DAY, PUSHING A BUTTON AND NOT HAVING TO WORRY ABOUT DINNER UNTIL IT'S TIME TO EAT JUST MAKES THE DAY FEEL MORE MANAGEABLE. AND IF WE CAN GIVE YOU THE GIFT OF LESS STRESS, WE'LL COUNT THAT AS A WIN.

OF COURSE, SLOW COOKING CAN ALSO BE A WHOLE LOT OF FUN — AND EVEN A LITTLE BIT FANCY. FOR EVERY STANDBY HEARTY STEW (WHICH SLOW COOKERS HAVE BECOME KNOWN FOR), THERE'S A NIFTY LITTLE APPETIZER OR DESSERT RECIPE THAT SLOW COOKERS CAN BE CALLED INTO SERVICE TO MAKE, WHETHER YOU WANT A GOOEY, CHEESY DIP THAT WILL STAY WARM THROUGHOUT YOUR PARTY OR PERFECTLY COOKED POTS DE CRÈME, GENTLY STEAMED ON YOUR COUNTERTOP, TO IMPRESS DINNER GUESTS.

IN CLASSIC BRIDGE FASHION (AND AS THE NEW GROUP OF LADIES, WE BOW DOWN TO BRIDGE TRADITION AND STRIVE TO HONOR THE HUMOR AND VERVE OF THE ORIGINAL LADIES), WE WANT YOU TO HAVE FUN WITH THESE RECIPES, HAVE A LAUGH OR TWO (OR 20) WITH FRIENDS AND FAMILY AS YOU GATHER TO COOK AND EAT, AND (FINGERS CROSSED) MAKE THE RECIPES PART OF YOUR OWN KITCHEN REPERTOIRE.

IF THE TIME-SAVER THAT IS THE SLOW COOKER MEANS YOU HAVE MORE HOURS IN THE DAY TO GET WHATEVER YOU NEED TO DO DONE (EVEN IF IT'S CATCHING UP ON GOSSIP OR POURING YOURSELF A GLASS OF WINE), WE'VE DONE OUR JOB.

HAPPY SLOW COOKING!

— JULIE, ELIZABETH AND SUE

SO YOU WANT TO DO SOME SLOW COOKING

IN A CLASSIC CASE OF WHAT'S OLD IS NEW AGAIN, SLOW COOKERS SEEM TO BE ALL THE RAGE THESE DAYS (WHICH PROVES THAT YOU SHOULD NEVER THROW ANYTHING OUT — HOW MANY OF US HAD TO BUY TWISTER FOR THE SECOND TIME?). IN THE QUEST TO STREAMLINE LIFE A LITTLE BIT, WE'RE REDISCOVERING OLD RECIPES AND ADAPTING FAMILY FAVORITES TO WORK IN THE SLOW COOKER. EVEN IF YOU'RE NOT LOOKING FOR RECIPES THAT YOU CAN DUMP INTO THE SLOW COOKER IN THE MORNING TO COME HOME TO AFTER WORK, SLOW COOKERS COME IN HANDY WHEN YOU'RE PUTTERING AROUND THE HOUSE ON A WEEKEND, OR HOSTING A BIG FAMILY DINNER AND HAVE LIMITED ROOM IN THE OVEN. THEY ALSO MAKE SUMMER COOKING A BREEZE: NO MORE HEATING UP THE ENTIRE HOUSE IN ORDER TO GET A HOT MEAL ON THE TABLE!

THAT SAID, THERE'S A COMMON MISCONCEPTION THAT SLOW COOKERS ARE SOMEHOW FOOLPROOF. ANYONE CAN USE A SLOW COOKER, BUT IT'S NOT SOME KIND OF MAGICAL ROBOT CHEF THAT WILL ABSOLVE YOU OF ANY CULINARY RESPONSIBILITIES (THAT'S WHAT TAKEOUT IS FOR). TO HELP ENSURE THAT THINGS TURN OUT THE WAY YOU WANT THEM TO, HERE ARE A FEW TIPS TO HELP YOU GET TO KNOW YOUR WAY AROUND A SLOW COOKER:

FIRST OFF, THERE ARE A LOT OF VARIATIONS WHEN IT COMES TO DIFFERENT MODELS. WHETHER YOU'RE DUSTING OFF A VINTAGE SLOW COOKER YOU INHERITED WHEN YOUR PARENTS DOWNSIZED OR BUYING A FANCY NEW ONE WITH MULTIPLE

COOKING TEMPERATURES AND TIMER OPTIONS, YOUR MACHINE IS GOING TO HAVE ITS OWN SPECIAL QUIRKS.

THERE IS NO UNIVERSAL STANDARD FOR HOW HOT THE HIGH AND LOW SETTINGS ARE, SO COOKING TIMES CAN VARY ENORMOUSLY BETWEEN MODELS. IF YOU HAVE A NEW SLOW COOKER, OR IT'S BEEN A LONG TIME SINCE YOU'VE USED ONE, WE SUGGEST YOU PLAN ON BEING HOME THE FIRST FEW TIMES YOU USE IT SO YOU CAN CHECK ON THINGS FROM TIME TO TIME. AS YOU GET TO KNOW ITS PERSONALITY (GO AHEAD, GIVE IT A NAME IF YOU'D LIKE — OURS ARE CALLED "MARY," "HELEN" AND "VAL"), YOU CAN LEAVE IT TO DO ITS THING MORE AND MORE.

WHEN YOU'RE FOLLOWING A RECIPE, KEEP IN MIND THAT THE COOKING TIMES ARE ONLY ESTIMATES, AND WE USUALLY GIVE A FAIRLY WIDE RANGE. IT'S A GOOD IDEA TO CHECK AT THE START OF THE ESTIMATED TIME, OR EVEN EARLIER IF YOU KNOW YOUR SLOW COOKER RUNS PARTICULARLY HOT. IN THE OLD DAYS, SLOW COOKER RECIPES WERE ALWAYS GIVEN AN 8-HOUR COOKING TIME, PRESUMING THE COOK WAS AT WORK FOR THE DAY OR IN BED FOR THE NIGHT. TASTES HAVE CHANGED OVER THE LAST FEW DECADES, AND WE'RE GENERALLY NOT AS TOLERANT OF OVERCOOKED FOOD AS WE ONCE WERE — WHAT MIGHT HAVE TASTED JUST RIGHT IN 1978 MAY FEEL MUSHY AND DRAINED OF FLAVOR TO A NEW-MILLENNIUM PALATE.

YOU MAY HAVE READ THAT YOU WANT TO AVOID LIFTING THE LID OF YOUR SLOW COOKER BEFORE YOU'RE SURE THAT THE FOOD IS DONE. WE AGREE, BUT ONLY TO A POINT. YOU CAN CERTAINLY TAKE A QUICK PEEK NOW AND AGAIN, BUT DO AVOID LOOKING WHEN YOU KNOW YOU DON'T NEED TO, OR LEAVING

THE LID OFF FOR MORE THAN A SECOND OR TWO (UNLESS, OF COURSE, THE RECIPE ADVISES YOU TO DO SO). SLOW COOKER PROS SAY EACH TIME YOU TAKE THE LID OFF, IT ADDS ABOUT 20 MINUTES OF COOKING TIME, AS ALL THAT WARM STEAM ESCAPES AND THE HEAT MUST ACCUMULATE AGAIN.

THINKING OF BUYING A SLOW COOKER? THERE'S A HUGE RANGE OUT THERE, AND COST IS NOT USUALLY MUCH OF AN INDICATION OF OVERALL FUNCTIONALITY. IF YOU'RE GOING TO OWN ONLY ONE SLOW COOKER, A 5- TO 6-QUART OVAL MIGHT BE YOUR MOST VERSATILE OPTION. WE LOVE BEING ABLE TO PROGRAM A TIME AND HAVE THE SLOW COOKER SWITCH ITSELF TO THE WARM SETTING WHEN IT'S DONE. A CLEAR GLASS LID — WHICH MOST HAVE NOWADAYS — MEANS YOU CAN SEE HOW THINGS ARE GOING WITHOUT LIFTING THE LID (SORT OF — IT WILL STEAM UP). APART FROM THESE PERKS, WE SUGGEST YOU TAKE A LOOK AT CURRENT PRODUCT REVIEWS AND FIND OUT WHAT OTHER PEOPLE ARE HAPPY WITH. OR BORROW A SLOW COOKER FROM A FRIEND AND GIVE IT A TEST-DRIVE!

SOME SLOW COOKER BOOKS GIVE YOU COOKING TIMES FOR BOTH THE LOW AND HIGH SETTINGS. WE DIDN'T DO THAT BECAUSE WE BELIEVE THAT MEATS AND STEWS THAT ARE MEANT TO BE SLOW-COOKED OVER LONG PERIODS OF TIME SHOULD BE GIVEN THAT LONGER TIME AT A LOWER TEMPERATURE TO HELP THE MEAT BREAK DOWN PROPERLY AND GIVE THE FLAVORS TIME TO MINGLE — COOKING IT TWICE AS FAST ON HIGH SIMPLY WON'T HAVE THE SAME EFFECT. ON THE OTHER HAND, A FEW OF THE RECIPES IN THE BOOK, PARTICULARLY CAKES AND RICE DISHES, CALL SPECIFICALLY FOR THE HIGH SETTING, AND WE'D RECOMMEND YOU STICK WITH THAT.

YOU'LL ALSO NOTICE THAT THE COOKING TIMES ON SOME OF THE RECIPES ARE SHORTER THAN YOU'D EXPECT FROM A TRADITIONAL SLOW COOKER BOOK. IF IT'S A STEW OR MEAT DISH THAT NEEDS TO COOK FOR 8 HOURS AND YOU EXPECT TO BE OUT FOR 10 HOURS, SET YOUR SLOW COOKER TO THE APPROPRIATE TIME AND IT SHOULD BE FINE ON WARM UNTIL YOU GET HOME. BUT YOU'RE NOT GOING TO BE ABLE TO GET AWAY WITH THIS ON SOMETHING THAT NEEDS TO COOK FOR ONLY 3 OR 4 HOURS. SAVE RECIPES WITH SHORTER COOKING TIMES FOR WEEKENDS, OR DAYS WHEN YOU KNOW YOU'LL BE IN AND OUT OF THE HOUSE AND CAN PUT YOUR SLOW COOKER ON LATER IN THE DAY AND BE AROUND TO KEEP AN EYE ON IT.

FROZEN ASSETS

ONE BENEFIT OF USING THE SLOW COOKER IS THAT IT'S PERFECT FOR PREPARING LARGE BATCHES OF SOUPS, STEWS, CHILI AND OTHER DISHES THAT FREEZE PARTICULARLY WELL. BECAUSE THEY'VE ALREADY BROKEN DOWN OVER TIME IN THE SLOW COOKER, THE FOODS' CONSISTENCY WON'T CHANGE ONCE THEY'VE BEEN FROZEN AND THAWED. (THE EXCEPTION TO THIS RULE IS WHITE POTATOES, WHICH TEND TO SEPARATE AND BECOME WATERY AFTER THEY'VE BEEN FROZEN.) ANY DISH THAT HAS A HIGH QUANTITY OF LIQUID WILL ALSO HAVE STAYING POWER — THE STOCK OR SAUCE ACTS AS INSULATION FOR MEAT AND OTHER INGREDIENTS, PROTECTING THEM FROM FREEZER BURN.

TO FREEZE LEFTOVERS — OR IF YOU LIKE COOKING IN LARGE BATCHES OR WANT TO PLAN AHEAD AND HAVE MEALS

STASHED AWAY FOR NIGHTS WHEN YOU DON'T HAVE TIME TO COOK — FIRST LET YOUR DISH COOL COMPLETELY, THEN FREEZE IT IN PORTIONS THAT SUIT YOUR NEEDS. SLICING LARGE ITEMS, LIKE POT ROAST, WILL MAKE THEM EASIER TO PACKAGE UP AND FREEZE. FREEZER CONTAINERS AND BAGS WORK WELL (BONUS: BAGS WILL LIE FLAT, FREEZE FAST AND BE STACKABLE). THE SMALLER THE CONTAINER, THE MORE QUICKLY YOUR FOOD WILL FREEZE AND THAW. INDIVIDUAL PORTIONS ARE PERFECT FOR GRABBING TO TAKE TO WORK FOR LUNCH, OR FOR REHEATING WHEN YOU'RE NOT SURE WHO WILL BE HOME FOR DINNER WHEN. JUST REMEMBER TO ALLOW ROOM FOR YOUR FOOD TO EXPAND AS IT FREEZES — AND AVOID GLASS JARS, WHICH COULD CRACK.

DON'T FORGET TO LABEL YOUR CONTAINERS. WE ALWAYS THINK WE'LL REMEMBER WHAT WE'VE PUT AWAY IN THE FREEZER, AND THEN IT TURNS INTO A GAME OF DINNERTIME FROZEN FOOD ROULETTE!

BREAKFAST & BRUNCH

SLOW COOKER SCHWARTIES

OUR FAMOUS SCHWARTIES POTATOES, SLOW COOKER STYLE!

¼ CUP	GRATED ONION	60 ML
2 LBS	FROZEN DICED HASH BROWNS	1 KG
2	CANS (EACH 10 OZ/284 ML) CONDENSED CREAM OF MUSHROOM SOUP	2
2 CUPS	SHREDDED CHEDDAR CHEESE	500 ML
2 CUPS	SOUR CREAM	500 ML
½ CUP	BUTTER, MELTED	125 ML
	SALT TO TASTE	

COMBINE ALL INGREDIENTS IN A 6-QUART SLOW COOKER. COVER AND COOK ON LOW FOR 6 TO 8 HOURS OR UNTIL THE CASSEROLE IS BROWN AROUND THE EDGES. THE FAT WILL SEPARATE AND FLOAT TO THE TOP DURING COOKING; GIVE IT A GOOD STIR TO REINTEGRATE BEFORE SERVING. SERVES 8 TO 10.

TIP: LEFTOVER SCHWARTIES CAN BE TURNED INTO SCHWARTIES PANCAKES. COMBINE 3 TO 4 CUPS (750 ML TO 1 L) LEFTOVER SCHWARTIES POTATOES WITH 2 LIGHTLY BEATEN LARGE EGGS AND ½ CUP (125 ML) ALL-PURPOSE FLOUR. FORM INTO PATTIES AND FRY IN A SKILLET WITH A DRIZZLE OF VEGETABLE OIL.

BACON CHEDDAR BREAKFAST POTATOES

THIS RECIPE GETS MAXIMUM FLAVOR OUT OF ONLY A FEW SLICES OF BACON. IT'S A GREAT WAY TO HELP FEED A CROWD OF TEENAGERS (OR RELATIVES!) AFTER A SLEEPOVER WITHOUT BREAKING THE BANK. SET YOUR SLOW COOKER ON A TIMER BEFORE YOU GO TO BED AND YOU'LL HAVE ALMOST NO FUSS IN THE MORNING.

4 to 6	BACON SLICES, CHOPPED	4 to 6
2 LBS	CHOPPED RED OR YELLOW POTATOES (NO NEED TO PEEL)	1 KG
4 to 6	GREEN ONIONS, SLICED	4 to 6
	SALT TO TASTE	
1/2 CUP	SHREDDED CHEDDAR CHEESE	125 ML

IN A MEDIUM SKILLET, SAUTÉ BACON UNTIL IT STARTS TO CRISP. USING A SLOTTED SPOON, TRANSFER BACON TO A 4- TO 6-QUART SLOW COOKER. STIR IN POTATOES, GREEN ONIONS AND SALT, THEN COVER AND COOK ON LOW FOR 5 TO 7 HOURS OR UNTIL POTATOES ARE TENDER. SCATTER CHEESE OVER EVERYTHING, TOSS TO COMBINE AND REPLACE THE LID FOR 10 MINUTES. SERVES 6.

"LIFE EXPECTANCY WOULD GROW BY LEAPS AND BOUNDS IF GREEN VEGETABLES SMELLED AS GOOD AS BACON."
— DOUG LARSON

SWEET POTATO AND PASTRAMI HASH

SERVE THIS HASH ALONGSIDE OTHER BRUNCH (OR EVEN DINNER) DISHES OR THROW A COUPLE OF POACHED OR FRIED EGGS ON TOP AND CALL IT A MEAL.

3	MEDIUM SWEET POTATOES, PEELED AND CUT INTO 1/4-INCH (0.5 CM) CUBES	3
2	GARLIC CLOVES, MINCED	2
1	ONION, CHOPPED	1
1	CAN (14 OZ/398 ML) DICED TOMATOES, DRAINED	1
1 CUP	CHOPPED PASTRAMI	250 ML
1 TBSP	WORCESTERSHIRE SAUCE	15 ML
1/2 TSP	DRIED THYME	2 ML
PINCH	SALT	PINCH
PINCH	BLACK PEPPER	PINCH

COMBINE ALL INGREDIENTS IN A 4- TO 6-QUART SLOW COOKER. COVER AND COOK ON LOW FOR 5 TO 6 HOURS OR UNTIL SWEET POTATOES ARE TENDER. SERVES 4 TO 6.

TIP: IF YOU PREFER A CRISPIER HASH, HEAT SOME VEGETABLE OIL IN A SKILLET SET OVER MEDIUM-HIGH HEAT. USE A SLOTTED SPOON TO TRANSFER THE HASH TO THE HOT PAN. FRY UNTIL CRISPY, SEASON WITH SALT AND PEPPER TO TASTE AND SERVE IMMEDIATELY.

BREAKFAST SAUSAGE AND BEANS

BEANS ARE A GREAT WAY TO STRETCH A SMALL
QUANTITY OF MEAT TO FEED A CROWD. THIS DISH HOLDS
WELL FOR A COUPLE OF HOURS ON THE WARM SETTING
OF YOUR SLOW COOKER. IF YOU FIND THE SAUCE IS
STARTING TO THICKEN AND DRY MORE THAN YOU LIKE,
JUST STIR IN A LITTLE WATER TO THIN IT OUT.

1 to 2 LBS	ENGLISH BANGERS (OR SAUSAGES OF YOUR CHOICE)	500 G to 1 KG
3	CANS (EACH 19 OZ/540 ML) BEANS, RINSED AND DRAINED (6 CUPS/1.5 L)	3
1	SMALL ONION, FINELY CHOPPED	1
1/2 CUP	PURE MAPLE SYRUP	125 ML
1/2 CUP	KETCHUP	125 ML
1/4 CUP	TOMATO PASTE	60 ML
2 TBSP	MOLASSES (ANY KIND)	30 ML
2 TBSP	DIJON MUSTARD	30 ML

SQUEEZE SAUSAGES FROM THEIR CASING INTO A LARGE
SKILLET SET OVER MEDIUM-HIGH HEAT. COOK, BREAKING
UP THE LARGER PIECES, UNTIL BROWNED. DISCARD ANY
ACCUMULATED FAT. TRANSFER MEAT TO A 6-QUART SLOW
COOKER AND STIR IN ALL REMAINING INGREDIENTS. COVER
AND COOK ON LOW FOR 6 TO 8 HOURS. SERVES 8 TO 10
(OR MORE AS PART OF A BUFFET).

TIP: FOR THE BEANS, TRY BLACK BEANS, KIDNEY BEANS,
BLACK-EYED PEAS OR A COMBINATION.

SAVORY SPINACH AND CHEDDAR BREAD PUDDING

THIS SAVORY BREAD DISH IS PERFECT FOR MIDDAY BRUNCH GET-TOGETHERS.

	NONSTICK COOKING SPRAY	
1	BUNCH SPINACH (ABOUT 10 OZ/300 G), TRIMMED AND CHOPPED	1
8 CUPS	CUBED DAY-OLD SOURDOUGH BREAD	2 L
1 CUP	SHREDDED CHEDDAR CHEESE	250 ML
4	LARGE EGGS, LIGHTLY BEATEN	4
2	GARLIC CLOVES, MINCED	2
2 CUPS	MILK	500 ML
1/4 CUP	BUTTER, MELTED	60 ML
1 TBSP	DIJON MUSTARD	15 ML
	SALT AND BLACK PEPPER TO TASTE	

SPRAY THE BOWL OF A 4- TO 6-QUART SLOW COOKER WITH COOKING SPRAY. IN A LARGE BOWL, TOSS TOGETHER SPINACH, BREAD CUBES AND CHEESE. IN ANOTHER BOWL, WHISK TOGETHER EGGS, GARLIC, MILK, BUTTER, MUSTARD, SALT AND PEPPER. POUR EGG MIXTURE OVER BREAD MIXTURE AND PRESS BREAD DOWN SO IT'S COMPLETELY SUBMERGED. LET STAND FOR 15 TO 30 MINUTES SO THE BREAD CAN ABSORB THE EGG.

TRANSFER BREAD MIXTURE AND ANY LIQUID LEFT IN THE BOTTOM OF THE BOWL TO THE SLOW COOKER. COVER AND COOK ON LOW FOR 3 1/2 TO 4 1/2 HOURS OR UNTIL PUDDING IS SET. SERVES 4 TO 6.

SPANISH TORTILLA

TORTILLA ESPAÑOLA IS FOUND EVERYWHERE IN SPAIN AND CAN BE SERVED EITHER HOT OR COLD. THE CHEESE IN OUR VERSION ISN'T TRADITIONAL (DON'T TELL!), BUT IS USED TO SUBTLY ENHANCE THE FLAVOR RATHER THAN MAKE A BIG CHEESY STATEMENT.

1	SMALL ONION, SLICED	1
2 TBSP	OLIVE OIL	30 ML
8	LARGE EGGS	8
3 CUPS	FROZEN SHREDDED HASH BROWNS, THAWED	750 ML
1/2 CUP	SHREDDED CHEDDAR CHEESE	125 ML
1/2 TSP	SALT	2 ML

LINE THE BOWL OF A 4- TO 6-QUART SLOW COOKER WITH PARCHMENT PAPER, PRESSING IT UP AGAINST THE SIDES WHERE IT FOLDS NATURALLY (IT DOESN'T NEED TO BE PERFECT). SOME OF THE POINTS WILL BE TALLER THAN THE RIM; LEAVE IT THAT WAY FOR NOW.

IN A SMALL DISH, MICROWAVE ONION AND OIL ON HIGH FOR 3 TO 4 MINUTES OR UNTIL ONION IS SOFTENED. LET COOL.

IN A LARGE BOWL, USE A FORK TO BEAT EGGS JUST UNTIL YOLKS ARE BARELY COMBINED WITH WHITES. STIR IN ONION (SCRAPE THE OIL IN AS WELL), HASH BROWNS, CHEESE AND SALT. POUR INTO PREPARED SLOW COOKER. TRIM THE PARCHMENT LEVEL WITH THE RIM OF THE BOWL. COVER AND COOK ON LOW FOR 2 TO 3 HOURS OR UNTIL EGG IS JUST BARELY SET IN THE CENTER. CAREFULLY LIFT PARCHMENT ONTO A PLATE, THEN CUT TORTILLA INTO WEDGES. SERVES 6.

HUEVOS RANCHEROS

THIS RECIPE IS AT LEAST ONE OF OUR HUSBANDS'
FAVORITE WAY TO HAVE EGGS ON A LAZY WEEKEND
MORNING. SERVE WITH WARMED TORTILLAS, GUACAMOLE,
SOUR CREAM AND OTHER MEXICAN-INSPIRED TOPPINGS
IF YOU WANT TO STRETCH THIS OUT TO FEED A CROWD!

I	BUNCH GREEN ONIONS, SLICED	I
2 TBSP	VEGETABLE OIL	30 ML
1$\frac{3}{4}$ CUPS	TOMATO SALSA (OR A 15-OZ/ 430 ML JAR)	425 ML
12	LARGE EGGS	12
I	CAN (19 OZ/540 ML) PINTO, RED KIDNEY OR BLACK BEANS, RINSED AND DRAINED (2 CUPS/500 ML)	I
$\frac{3}{4}$ CUP	DICED CHEDDAR OR MONTEREY JACK CHEESE	175 ML
	SALT AND BLACK PEPPER TO TASTE	

LINE THE BOWL OF A 4- TO 6-QUART SLOW COOKER WITH
PARCHMENT PAPER, PRESSING IT UP AGAINST THE SIDES
WHERE IT FOLDS NATURALLY (IT DOESN'T NEED TO BE
PERFECT). SOME OF THE POINTS WILL BE TALLER THAN
THE RIM; LEAVE IT THAT WAY FOR NOW.

IN A SMALL DISH, MICROWAVE GREEN ONIONS AND OIL
ON HIGH FOR ABOUT 2 MINUTES OR UNTIL SOFTENED; SET
ASIDE. DRAIN SALSA IN A FINE-MESH STRAINER SET OVER
A BOWL WHILE YOU COOK THE EGGS.

IN A LARGE BOWL, USE A FORK TO BEAT EGGS JUST
UNTIL YOLKS ARE BARELY COMBINED WITH WHITES. STIR
IN GREEN ONIONS (SCRAPE THE OIL IN AS WELL), BEANS,
CHEESE, SALT AND PEPPER. POUR INTO PREPARED SLOW

COOKER. TRIM THE PARCHMENT LEVEL WITH THE RIM OF THE BOWL. COVER AND COOK ON HIGH FOR 40 TO 60 MINUTES OR UNTIL EGG IS SET AROUND THE EDGES AND ABOUT HALFWAY TO THE MIDDLE. STIR WITH A RUBBER SPATULA JUST ENOUGH TO LIFT THE COOKED PORTIONS OF EGG INTO THE MIDDLE AND BREAK THEM UP SLIGHTLY. COVER AND COOK FOR 5 MINUTES LONGER.

DISCARD THE JUICE FROM THE STRAINED SALSA. ADD SALSA TO THE EGG MIXTURE AND JUST BARELY FOLD IT IN SO AS NOT TO BREAK UP THE EGG TOO MUCH. SERVES 6 TO 10.

PROMISES AND PIE CRUSTS ARE MADE TO BE BROKEN.
— JONATHAN SWIFT

SHAKSHUKA

VARIATIONS ON THIS SPICY DISH ARE FOUND THROUGHOUT THE MIDDLE EAST, AND IT MAKES A WONDERFUL BREAKFAST, LUNCH OR SUPPER. WHILE THE EGGS ARE USUALLY POACHED RIGHT IN THE PAN, WE FIND IT EASIER TO POACH OR FRY THEM SEPARATELY. SERVE WITH CRUSTY BREAD OR PITA ALONGSIDE.

5	GARLIC CLOVES, MINCED	5
2 to 3	JALAPEÑO PEPPERS, SEEDED AND FINELY CHOPPED	2 to 3
2	RED BELL PEPPERS, SLICED	2
1	GREEN BELL PEPPER, SLICED	1
1	LARGE ONION, CUT IN HALF AND THINLY SLICED	1
1	CAN (28 OZ/796 ML) DICED TOMATOES, WITH JUICE	1
1	CAN (14 OZ/398 ML) DICED TOMATOES, WITH JUICE	1
1	CAN (5$\frac{1}{2}$ OZ/156 ML) TOMATO PASTE	1
1$\frac{1}{2}$ TBSP	PAPRIKA	22 ML
1$\frac{1}{2}$ TBSP	GROUND CUMIN	22 ML
	SALT AND BLACK PEPPER TO TASTE	
	POACHED OR FRIED EGGS (1 OR 2 PER PERSON)	
	CRUMBLED FETA CHEESE	
	CHOPPED FRESH CILANTRO	

COMBINE GARLIC, JALAPEÑOS TO TASTE, RED PEPPERS, GREEN PEPPER, ONION, TOMATOES, TOMATO PASTE, PAPRIKA, CUMIN, SALT AND PEPPER IN A 4- TO 6-QUART SLOW COOKER. COVER AND COOK ON LOW FOR 7 TO 9 HOURS OR UNTIL VEGETABLES ARE VERY SOFT.

SERVE IN SHALLOW BOWLS, WITH AN EGG OR TWO PERCHED ON TOP OF EACH SERVING, ALONG WITH SOME FETA AND CILANTRO. SERVES 6.

BAKED EGGS

THE YOLKS COOK AT A SIMILAR RATE TO THE WHITES WHEN YOU BAKE EGGS — EXPECT A SLIGHTLY FIRM, ALMOST VELVETY TEXTURE. YOU CAN KEEP EXTRAS IN THE FRIDGE FOR A DAY OR TWO.

	BUTTER	
1/3 CUP	HEAVY OR WHIPPING (35%) CREAM	75 ML
12	LARGE EGGS	12
	SALT AND BLACK PEPPER TO TASTE	
	FRESH THYME LEAVES, SLIVERS OF FRESH BASIL OR FINELY CHOPPED PARSLEY (OPTIONAL)	
1/3 CUP	GRATED PARMESAN CHEESE	75 ML

BUTTER SIX 6-OZ (175 ML) RAMEKINS AND POUR A LITTLE CREAM INTO EACH, DIVIDING IT EVENLY. CRACK 2 EGGS INTO EACH RAMEKIN AND SPRINKLE WITH SALT AND PEPPER. TOP WITH FRESH HERBS (IF YOU'RE USING THEM) AND PARMESAN. POUR 1 1/2 CUPS (375 ML) WATER INTO A 6-QUART SLOW COOKER. PLACE 3 RAMEKINS IN THE WATER, THEN PLACE THE REMAINING 3 ON TOP, RESTING THEM ON THE RIMS OF THE LOWER ONES. COVER AND COOK ON HIGH FOR 1 TO 1 3/4 HOURS OR UNTIL EGGS ARE COOKED. SERVES 6.

CINNAMON ROLL CASSEROLE

ADD THIS MONKEY BREAD CREATION TO A BRUNCH TABLE AND YOU'LL BE AMAZED BY HOW QUICKLY IT GETS EATEN. THIS RECIPE CAN ALSO BE MADE WITH A 16.3-OZ (462 G) TUBE OF CINNAMON ROLL DOUGH (DISCARD THE ICING PACKET AND USE OUR TOPPING AND ICING), BUT IT'S SO MUCH MORE SATISFYING TO DO IT FROM SCRATCH.

DOUGH

2 1/2 TSP	ACTIVE DRY YEAST	12 ML
1/2 CUP	WARM WATER	125 ML
3 CUPS	ALL-PURPOSE FLOUR, DIVIDED	750 ML
1/4 CUP	SUGAR	60 ML
I TSP	SALT	5 ML
I	LARGE EGG	I
1/2 CUP	MILK	125 ML
2 TBSP	BUTTER, SOFTENED	30 ML

FILLING

2 TBSP	SUGAR	30 ML
2 TSP	GROUND CINNAMON	10 ML
I TBSP	BUTTER, SOFTENED	15 ML

TOPPING

1/2 CUP	PACKED BROWN SUGAR	125 ML
I TSP	GROUND CINNAMON	5 ML
1/4 CUP	BUTTER, MELTED	60 ML
	NONSTICK COOKING SPRAY	
1/2 CUP	CHOPPED PECANS	125 ML

ICING

2 TBSP	BUTTER	30 ML
2 TBSP	WATER	30 ML
I CUP	POWDERED (ICING) SUGAR	250 ML

DOUGH: IN A LARGE BOWL, SPRINKLE YEAST OVER WARM WATER; LET STAND FOR 1 TO 2 MINUTES OR UNTIL FOAMY. (IF IT DOESN'T GET FOAMY, IT'S INACTIVE; TOSS IT AND BUY SOME FRESH YEAST!) ADD HALF THE FLOUR ALONG WITH THE SUGAR, SALT, EGG, MILK AND BUTTER; STIR UNTIL WELL BLENDED AND STICKY. ADD THE REMAINING FLOUR, STIRRING UNTIL THE DOUGH COMES TOGETHER. KNEAD FOR 5 TO 6 MINUTES OR UNTIL SMOOTH AND ELASTIC. COVER WITH A TEA TOWEL AND LET RISE FOR $1\frac{1}{2}$ HOURS OR UNTIL DOUBLED IN BULK.

FILLING: IN A BOWL, COMBINE SUGAR AND CINNAMON. ON A LIGHTLY FLOURED SURFACE, ROLL DOUGH INTO A 15- BY 10-INCH (38 BY 25 CM) RECTANGLE. SPREAD WITH BUTTER AND SPRINKLE WITH CINNAMON SUGAR. STARTING ON A LONG SIDE, ROLL DOUGH UP LIKE A JELLY ROLL. CUT INTO 6 PIECES, THEN CUT EACH PIECE INTO 6 CHUNKS.

TOPPING: IN A SMALL BOWL, COMBINE BROWN SUGAR, CINNAMON AND BUTTER. SPRAY THE BOWL OF A 4- TO 6-QUART SLOW COOKER WITH COOKING SPRAY. ADD HALF THE CINNAMON ROLL PIECES. TOP WITH HALF THE BROWN SUGAR MIXTURE, THEN HALF THE PECANS. REPEAT LAYERS. COVER AND COOK ON LOW FOR 2 TO 3 HOURS OR UNTIL ROLLS ARE FULLY BAKED.

ICING: IN A SMALL SAUCEPAN, HEAT BUTTER AND WATER OVER MEDIUM HEAT UNTIL BUTTER MELTS. WHISK IN POWDERED SUGAR.

CAREFULLY INVERT THE SLOW COOKER BOWL OVER A PLATE SO THE CINNAMON ROLLS SLIDE OUT. DRIZZLE WITH ICING AND SERVE WARM. SERVES 8 TO 10.

FRENCH TOAST WITH BLUEBERRY SAUCE

LETTING FRENCH TOAST COOK SLOWLY RATHER THAN FRYING IT ON A GRIDDLE GIVES IT A RICH, CUSTARDY FLAVOR. BECAUSE IT TAKES 4 HOURS TO COOK, THIS RECIPE IS PERFECT FOR MIDDAY BRUNCHES.

TOAST

	NONSTICK COOKING SPRAY	
1	LARGE LOAF DAY-OLD FRENCH BREAD	1
8	LARGE EGGS	8
2 CUPS	MILK (NOT SKIM)	500 ML
1/3 CUP	LIQUID HONEY	75 ML
1 CUP	FRESH OR FROZEN BLUEBERRIES	250 ML

SAUCE

1 CUP	SUGAR	250 ML
2 TBSP	CORNSTARCH	30 ML
1 CUP	FRESH OR FROZEN BLUEBERRIES	250 ML
1 CUP	WATER	250 ML
1 TBSP	BUTTER	15 ML

TOAST: SPRAY THE BOWL OF A 4- TO 6-QUART SLOW COOKER WITH COOKING SPRAY (A LARGE OVAL SLOW COOKER WORKS BEST HERE). CUT BREAD INTO THICK (ABOUT 3/4-INCH/2 CM) SLICES. CRACK EGGS INTO A MEDIUM BOWL AND BEAT LIGHTLY. WHISK IN MILK AND HONEY. LET EACH SLICE OF BREAD SOAK IN EGG MIXTURE FOR A FEW MOMENTS, THEN TRANSFER TO THE SLOW COOKER. ARRANGE HALF THE SLICES OF EGG-SOAKED BREAD, OVERLAPPING AS NECESSARY, ON THE BOTTOM OF THE SLOW COOKER, THEN SPRINKLE WITH BLUEBERRIES.

ARRANGE THE REMAINING BREAD SLICES ON TOP. COVER AND COOK ON LOW FOR $3\frac{1}{2}$ TO $4\frac{1}{2}$ HOURS OR UNTIL EGG IS SET.

SAUCE: IN A MEDIUM SAUCEPAN, STIR TOGETHER SUGAR AND CORNSTARCH. ADD BLUEBERRIES AND WATER; BRING TO A BOIL OVER MEDIUM-HIGH HEAT. REDUCE HEAT AND SIMMER, STIRRING OCCASIONALLY, FOR ABOUT 10 MINUTES OR UNTIL SYRUPY. STIR IN BUTTER UNTIL MELTED. SERVE WITH FRENCH TOAST. SERVES 6 TO 8.

VARIATIONS

MIXED BERRY SAUCE: THROW OTHER BERRIES, SUCH AS RASPBERRIES, STRAWBERRIES OR BLACKBERRIES, IN WITH THE BLUEBERRIES, USING A TOTAL OF 1 CUP (250 ML) BERRIES.

CINNAMON SAUCE: MELT $\frac{1}{3}$ CUP (75 ML) BUTTER IN A MEDIUM SAUCEPAN OVER MEDIUM HEAT. ADD 1 CUP (250 ML) PACKED BROWN SUGAR, $\frac{3}{4}$ CUP (175 ML) EVAPORATED MILK, $\frac{1}{4}$ CUP (60 ML) DARK CORN SYRUP AND 3 TBSP (45 ML) HOT WATER. CONTINUE COOKING, STIRRING CONSTANTLY, UNTIL THE SUGAR IS DISSOLVED. STIR IN 1 TBSP (15 ML) GROUND CINNAMON. SERVE IN PLACE OF THE BLUEBERRY SAUCE.

GIVE ME COFFEE TO CHANGE THE THINGS I CAN,
AND WINE TO ACCEPT THE THINGS I CAN'T!

OATMEAL WITH APRICOTS AND COCONUT MILK

IMAGINE WAKING UP TO A HOT BREAKFAST WITHOUT LIFTING A FINGER. SOUNDS LIKE A DREAM, DOESN'T IT?

	NONSTICK COOKING SPRAY	
2 CUPS	STEEL-CUT OATS	500 ML
I CUP	CHOPPED DRIED APRICOTS	250 ML
1/4 CUP	PACKED BROWN SUGAR	60 ML
I TSP	GROUND CINNAMON	5 ML
I TSP	SALT	5 ML
I	CAN (14 OZ/400 ML) COCONUT MILK	I
7 CUPS	WATER	1.75 L
	MILK OR CREAM	

SPRAY THE BOWL OF A 4- TO 6-QUART SLOW COOKER WITH COOKING SPRAY. COMBINE OATS, APRICOTS, BROWN SUGAR, CINNAMON, SALT AND COCONUT MILK IN THE SLOW COOKER. POUR IN WATER AND STIR TO COMBINE. COVER AND COOK ON LOW FOR 6 TO 8 HOURS OR HOWEVER LONG YOU PLAN TO SLEEP (SET A TIMER ON THE SLOW COOKER IF YOU TEND TO SLEEP IN).

GIVE THE OATMEAL A GOOD STIR, AS THE LIQUID AND OATS WILL SEPARATE OVERNIGHT AND MAY NOT LOOK PARTICULARLY APPETIZING. ONCE IT'S STIRRED AND LOOKING GOOD, THIN WITH MILK OR CREAM, IF NECESSARY. SERVES 6 TO 8.

TIP: SERVE WITH BROWN SUGAR AND MILK OR CREAM AND/OR TOPPINGS LIKE SHREDDED COCONUT OR SLICED ALMONDS.

TIP: UNLESS YOU HAVE A BIG FAMILY (OR A PARTICULARLY BIG APPETITE), YOU WILL HAVE LOADS OF LEFTOVERS. THE OATMEAL KEEPS WELL IN THE FRIDGE FOR A FEW DAYS AND CAN BE REHEATED IN THE MICROWAVE OR ON THE STOVETOP WITH A LITTLE BIT OF MILK TO KEEP IT FROM DRYING OUT. IF YOU WANT TO STRETCH IT EVEN FURTHER, FREEZE INDIVIDUAL PORTIONS IN MUFFIN TINS AND POP OUT TO REHEAT IN THE MICROWAVE FOR A QUICK AND EASY BREAKFAST.

VARIATIONS

APPLE CRANBERRY OATMEAL: OMIT THE APRICOTS AND ADD 2 CHOPPED PEELED APPLES AND $\frac{1}{2}$ CUP (125 ML) DRIED CRANBERRIES WITH THE OATS.

COCONUT BLUEBERRY OATMEAL: OMIT THE APRICOTS AND CINNAMON, AND ADD 1 CUP (250 ML) FROZEN BLUEBERRIES AND 1 TSP (5 ML) VANILLA WITH THE OATS. GARNISH WITH COCONUT FLAKES.

BANANA NUT OATMEAL: OMIT THE APRICOTS AND ADD 1 MASHED BANANA AND $\frac{1}{2}$ CUP (125 ML) CHOPPED NUTS (WALNUTS ARE A GOOD BET) WITH THE OATS. GARNISH WITH BANANA SLICES.

CHAI-SPICED OATMEAL

MASALA CHAI TRANSLATES TO "SPICED TEA." THE
FLAVORS HERE WILL MAKE YOUR MORNING BOWL OF
OATMEAL PARTICULARLY FRAGRANT AND WARMING —
A PLEASURE TO WAKE UP TO.

	NONSTICK COOKING SPRAY	
1 1/2 CUPS	STEEL-CUT OATS	375 ML
2 TBSP	PACKED BROWN SUGAR	30 ML
1 TSP	GROUND CARDAMOM	5 ML
1 TSP	GROUND CINNAMON	5 ML
1/2 TSP	GROUND GINGER	2 ML
1/8 TSP	GROUND FENNEL	0.5 ML
1/4 TSP	SALT	1 ML
2	PINCHES BLACK PEPPER	2
5 CUPS	WATER	1.25 L
1 CUP	STRONG BLACK TEA (SEE TIP)	250 ML

SPRAY THE BOWL OF A 4- TO 6-QUART SLOW COOKER WITH
COOKING SPRAY. COMBINE ALL INGREDIENTS IN THE SLOW
COOKER. COVER AND COOK ON LOW FOR 6 TO 8 HOURS
OR HOWEVER LONG YOU PLAN TO SLEEP (SET A TIMER
ON THE SLOW COOKER IF YOU TEND TO SLEEP IN). STIR
WITH A WOODEN SPOON OR HEATPROOF SPATULA (YOU'LL
NEED TO GET INTO THE CORNERS), THEN LET STAND FOR
10 MINUTES WITH THE LID OFF. SERVES 6.

TIP: THE BLACK TEA WILL GIVE THIS OATMEAL A SLIGHTLY
PEPPERY BITE. IF THAT DOESN'T SUIT YOU, REDUCE
THE TEA TO 1/2 CUP (125 ML) AND INCREASE THE WATER
TO 5 1/2 CUPS (1.375 L). OR, IF YOU'D RATHER AVOID THE
CAFFEINE IN BLACK TEA, YOU CAN USE A HERBAL TEA OR
WATER, KEEPING THE QUANTITIES THE SAME.

MARMALADE OATMEAL

ORANGES AND OATS GO BEAUTIFULLY TOGETHER, AND THE HOUSE WILL SMELL DELICIOUS WHEN YOU GET UP! WE LOVE USING OUR ORANGE MARMALADE (PAGE 267) FOR THIS.

	NONSTICK COOKING SPRAY	
1 1/2 CUPS	STEEL-CUT OATS	375 ML
1/2 CUP	ORANGE MARMALADE	125 ML
	FINELY GRATED ZEST OF 1 ORANGE	
1/4 TSP	SALT	1 ML
6 CUPS	WATER	1.5 L
2 TBSP	BUTTER, CUT INTO PIECES, OR COCONUT OIL	30 ML

SPRAY THE BOWL OF A 4- TO 6-QUART SLOW COOKER WITH NONSTICK SPRAY. COMBINE OATS, MARMALADE, ZEST, SALT AND WATER IN THE SLOW COOKER, STIRRING WELL. STIR IN BUTTER. COVER AND COOK ON LOW FOR 6 TO 8 HOURS OR HOWEVER LONG YOU PLAN TO SLEEP (SET A TIMER ON THE SLOW COOKER IF YOU TEND TO SLEEP IN). STIR WITH A WOODEN SPOON OR HEATPROOF SPATULA (YOU'LL NEED TO GET INTO THE CORNERS), THEN LET STAND FOR 10 MINUTES WITH THE LID OFF. SERVES 6.

TIP: SERVE AS IS OR WITH A DRIZZLE OF CREAM AND A SPOONFUL OF MARMALADE ON TOP.

ALMOND AND CHERRY GRANOLA

SLOW COOKING MAKES IT EASIER TO AVOID BURNT
GRANOLA THAN WITH TRADITIONAL OVEN VERSIONS.

I CUP	WHOLE ALMONDS	250 ML
5 CUPS	LARGE-FLAKE (OLD-FASHIONED) ROLLED OATS	1.25 L
I CUP	UNSWEETENED SHREDDED COCONUT	250 ML
1/2 CUP	PACKED BROWN SUGAR	125 ML
1/4 TSP	SALT	I ML
1/4 CUP	BUTTER	60 ML
I TBSP	VANILLA	15 ML
	NONSTICK COOKING SPRAY	
I CUP	DRIED TART CHERRIES	250 ML

COARSELY CHOP ALMONDS, AIMING TO CUT EACH ALMOND
INTO ONLY 2 OR 3 PIECES (SO THEY WON'T BURN AS
EASILY). IN A LARGE BOWL, COMBINE ALMONDS, OATS AND
COCONUT. IN A SMALL SAUCEPAN OVER MEDIUM HEAT,
STIR TOGETHER BROWN SUGAR, SALT AND BUTTER. BRING
JUST TO A BOIL, THEN REMOVE FROM HEAT AND LET
COOL FOR 2 MINUTES. STIR IN VANILLA. DRIZZLE BUTTER
MIXTURE OVER OAT MIXTURE, TOSSING UNTIL EVERYTHING
IS WELL COMBINED AND EVENLY COATED.

SPRAY THE BOWL OF A 4- TO 6-QUART SLOW COOKER
WITH COOKING SPRAY. POUR IN THE OAT MIXTURE.
COVER AND COOK ON HIGH FOR 30 TO 60 MINUTES OR
UNTIL GRANOLA IS HOT THROUGHOUT. STIR AND COOK,
UNCOVERED, ON HIGH FOR I TO 1 1/2 HOURS, STIRRING
EVERY SO OFTEN SO THE EDGES DON'T GET TOO BROWN.
TOWARD THE END OF THE COOKING TIME, YOU'LL NEED

TO STIR MORE OFTEN. ONCE EVERYTHING IS A COUPLE OF SHADES DARKER, STIR IN CHERRIES. TRANSFER TO A RIMMED BAKING SHEET AND LET COOL COMPLETELY. STORE IN A GLASS JAR AT ROOM TEMPERATURE FOR A FEW WEEKS. MAKES ABOUT 8 CUPS (2 L).

TIP: THE GRANOLA WILL TOAST A LITTLE FASTER IF YOU PUSH IT UP AGAINST THE SIDE OF THE SLOW COOKER, LEAVING A WELL IN THE MIDDLE.

VARIATIONS: GRANOLA ADAPTS WELL TO ALMOST ENDLESS VARIATIONS. TRY PECAN HALVES OR WHOLE HAZELNUTS IN PLACE OF THE ALMONDS, OR OTHER DRIED FRUITS, SUCH AS CRANBERRIES OR CHOPPED DRIED APRICOTS, INSTEAD OF THE TART CHERRIES. YOU CAN EVEN ADD CHUNKS OF DARK CHOCOLATE TO THE FINISHED (AND COMPLETELY COOLED) GRANOLA.

"A FRUIT IS A VEGETABLE WITH LOOKS AND MONEY.
PLUS, IF YOU LET FRUIT ROT, IT TURNS INTO WINE,
SOMETHING BRUSSELS SPROUTS NEVER DO."
— P. J. O'ROURKE

BREAKFAST BARLEY

BARLEY IS A WONDERFULLY VERSATILE GRAIN.
WE'VE KEPT IT SIMPLE HERE SO YOU CAN ADD
YOUR FAVORITE OATMEAL TOPPINGS.

	NONSTICK COOKING SPRAY	
1 CUP	POT OR PEARL BARLEY	250 ML
1 TSP	LIQUID HONEY	5 ML
1/4 TSP	GROUND ALLSPICE	1 ML
1	CINNAMON STICK	1
1/4 TSP	SALT	1 ML
4 CUPS	WATER	1 L

SPRAY THE BOWL OF A 4- TO 6-QUART SLOW COOKER
WITH COOKING SPRAY. COMBINE ALL INGREDIENTS IN THE
SLOW COOKER. COVER AND COOK ON LOW FOR 6 TO 8
HOURS OR HOWEVER LONG YOU PLAN TO SLEEP (SET A
TIMER ON THE SLOW COOKER IF YOU TEND TO SLEEP IN).
DISCARD CINNAMON STICK. STIR WITH A WOODEN SPOON
OR HEATPROOF SPATULA (YOU'LL NEED TO GET INTO THE
CORNERS), THEN LET STAND FOR 10 MINUTES WITH THE
LID OFF. SERVES 4 TO 6.

TIP: SERVE AS IS OR WITH FRESH OR DRIED FRUIT, CREAM
AND A DRIZZLE OF HONEY.

JUNK: SOMETHING YOU KEEP FOR YEARS, THEN THROW
AWAY 2 WEEKS BEFORE YOU NEED IT.

SNACKS & APPETIZERS

RETRO NUTS AND BOLTS

IT'S NOT A PARTY WITHOUT NUTS AND BOLTS — OR, AT LEAST, NOT A VERY GOOD ONE. THIS IS A CLASSIC, BUT ALSO AN OLD FAMILY RECIPE, GIVEN A KICK WITH SOME SPICY SEASONING.

4 CUPS	TOASTED RICE CEREAL SQUARES	1 L
3 CUPS	TOASTED OAT O'S CEREAL	750 ML
3 CUPS	CONE-SHAPED CRISPY CORN SNACKS (SUCH AS BUGLES)	750 ML
3 CUPS	PRETZEL STICKS	750 ML
2 CUPS	SALTED PEANUTS	500 ML
2 TSP	GARLIC POWDER	10 ML
1 TSP	CELERY SALT	5 ML
1 TSP	ONION POWDER	5 ML
1 CUP	BUTTER, MELTED	250 ML
3 TBSP	WORCESTERSHIRE SAUCE	45 ML

COMBINE CEREAL SQUARES, O'S CEREAL, CORN SNACKS, PRETZEL STICKS AND PEANUTS IN A 6-QUART SLOW COOKER. IN A SMALL BOWL, COMBINE GARLIC POWDER, CELERY SALT, ONION POWDER, BUTTER AND WORCESTERSHIRE SAUCE. POUR THE BUTTER MIXTURE OVER THE CEREAL MIX AND TOSS UNTIL AS EVENLY COATED AS POSSIBLE. COVER AND COOK ON HIGH FOR ABOUT 2 HOURS, STIRRING EVERY 15 MINUTES TO KEEP THE MIXTURE AT THE BOTTOM AND EDGES OF THE SLOW COOKER FROM BURNING. STORE IN AN AIRTIGHT CONTAINER AT ROOM TEMPERATURE FOR UP TO 2 WEEKS. MAKES ABOUT 15 CUPS (3.75 L).

TIP: THE SLOW COOKER WILL BE QUITE FULL AND SOME CEREAL MAY GO FLYING TO THE FLOOR — LUCKY DAY FOR THE DOG OR ANY SMALL CHILDREN ROAMING ABOUT!

TIP: DON'T WORRY TOO MUCH ABOUT WHAT CEREALS AND SNACKS YOU USE — IF YOU CAN'T FIND BUGLES OR PRETZEL STICKS, FEEL FREE TO USE CORN CHIPS OR MINI PRETZEL TWISTS. LIKEWISE, IF YOU'RE WORRIED ABOUT NUT ALLERGIES, JUST OMIT THE PEANUTS. THE KEY IS TO END UP WITH 15 CUPS (3.75 ML) OF DRY SNACKS TO GO WITH THE BUTTER AND SEASONING MIX.

LITTLE BOY TO POLICEMAN PARKING A VAN WITH
HIS K9 PARTNER BARKING IN THE BACK:
"IS THAT A DOG YOU GOT THERE?"
POLICEMAN: "YUP, SURE IS!"
LITTLE BOY: "WHAT'D HE DO?"

MAPLE PECAN SNACK MIX

SWEET, SPICY AND SALTY, THIS ADDICTIVE SNACK MIX HITS ALL THE RIGHT SPOTS.

4 CUPS	TOASTED RICE CEREAL SQUARES	1 L
3 CUPS	TOASTED OAT O'S CEREAL	750 ML
2 CUPS	PRETZEL STICKS	500 ML
2 CUPS	DRIED CRANBERRIES	500 ML
2 CUPS	PECAN HALVES	500 ML
1/4 CUP	PACKED BROWN SUGAR	60 ML
1 TBSP	GROUND CINNAMON	15 ML
1 TSP	GROUND ALLSPICE	5 ML
1/2 TSP	GROUND NUTMEG	2 ML
1/2 TSP	GROUND GINGER	2 ML
1/2 CUP	BUTTER, MELTED	125 ML
1/2 CUP	PURE MAPLE SYRUP	125 ML

COMBINE CEREAL SQUARES, O'S CEREAL, PRETZEL STICKS, CRANBERRIES AND PECANS IN A 6-QUART SLOW COOKER. IN A MEDIUM BOWL, COMBINE BROWN SUGAR, CINNAMON, ALLSPICE, NUTMEG, GINGER, BUTTER AND MAPLE SYRUP. POUR THE BUTTER MIXTURE OVER THE CEREAL MIXTURE AND STIR CAREFULLY UNTIL EVENLY COATED.

COVER AND COOK ON HIGH FOR 2 HOURS, STIRRING EVERY 15 MINUTES TO KEEP THE MIXTURE AT THE BOTTOM AND EDGES OF THE SLOW COOKER FROM BURNING. POUR THE SNACK MIX ONTO A BAKING SHEET, SPREAD OUT IN A SINGLE LAYER AND LET DRY FOR ABOUT 2 HOURS OR UNTIL NO LONGER STICKY. STORE IN AN AIRTIGHT CONTAINER AT ROOM TEMPERATURE FOR UP TO 2 WEEKS. MAKES ABOUT 13 CUPS (3.25 L).

BALSAMIC ROSEMARY PECANS

A BATCH OF SWEET AND SAVORY NUTS IS GOOD FOR GIFT GIVING, PARTY THROWING, SPONTANEOUS NIBBLING AND SALAD TOPPING.

3 CUPS	PECAN HALVES OR MIXED NUTS	750 ML
2 TBSP	PACKED BROWN SUGAR	30 ML
1 TBSP	CHOPPED FRESH ROSEMARY	15 ML
1/2 TSP	SALT	2 ML
1/4 TSP	BLACK PEPPER	1 ML
3 TBSP	BUTTER, MELTED	45 ML
2 TSP	BALSAMIC VINEGAR	10 ML
2	DROPS HOT PEPPER SAUCE	2

LINE A 4- TO 6-QUART SLOW COOKER WITH PARCHMENT PAPER, FOLDING IN OR CUTTING OFF THE POINTS OF PAPER, IF YOU LIKE. COMBINE ALL INGREDIENTS IN THE SLOW COOKER, STIRRING TO COAT THE NUTS WELL. COVER AND COOK ON HIGH FOR 1 HOUR. STIR, THEN COVER AND COOK ON LOW FOR 30 MINUTES, STIRRING ONCE OR TWICE. SPREAD OUT ON A PLATE OR BAKING SHEET TO COOL BEFORE SERVING OR STORING IN AN AIRTIGHT CONTAINER FOR UP TO 2 WEEKS. MAKES ABOUT 3 CUPS (750 ML).

HOT NUTZ

SPICY LIKE HOT WINGS, THESE CASHEWS LIVE UP TO THEIR NAME — EVEN IF YOU'RE NOT SERVING THEM WARM.

2 CUPS	CASHEWS	500 ML
1 TSP	GARLIC POWDER	5 ML
1/2 TSP	GROUND TURMERIC	2 ML
	SALT TO TASTE	
1/2 CUP	BUFFALO-STYLE HOT PEPPER SAUCE (SUCH AS FRANK'S REDHOT)	125 ML
1 TBSP	VEGETABLE OIL	15 ML

COMBINE ALL INGREDIENTS IN A 4- TO 6-QUART SLOW COOKER, THEN SPREAD OUT IN AN EVEN LAYER ALONG THE BOTTOM. COVER AND COOK ON HIGH FOR 1 HOUR. STIR, THEN COVER AND COOK ON LOW FOR 1 HOUR, STIRRING EVERY 20 MINUTES, UNTIL THE SAUCE HAS DRIED OUT. UNCOVER AND LET CASHEWS COOL IN THE SLOW COOKER UNTIL YOU'RE ABLE TO HANDLE THEM. SERVE IMMEDIATELY, WHILE STILL WARM, OR SPREAD OUT ON A BAKING SHEET TO COOL (THIS WILL ALSO LET THE CASHEWS DRY OUT A LITTLE BIT MORE). STORE IN AN AIRTIGHT CONTAINER AT ROOM TEMPERATURE FOR UP TO 1 WEEK. *MAKES ABOUT 2 CUPS (500 ML).*

EASY CHEESE FONDUE

A QUICK CHEESE FONDUE IS A GREAT WAY TO USE UP LEFTOVER CHEESE ENDS. WE LIKE IT BEST WITH A CLASSIC COMBINATION OF GRUYÈRE AND EMMENTAL. IF YOU'RE GOING SOMEWHERE, BRING IT TO REHEAT, ALONG WITH A LOAF OF CRUSTY BREAD AND A COUPLE OF TART APPLES TO SLICE AND DIP.

1	GARLIC CLOVE, PEELED AND HALVED LENGTHWISE	1
6 CUPS	SHREDDED GRUYÈRE AND/OR EMMENTAL CHEESE (1½ LBS/750 G)	1.5 L
3 TBSP	ALL-PURPOSE FLOUR	45 ML
1 TSP	DRY MUSTARD (OPTIONAL)	5 ML
1 CUP	BEER, DRY WHITE WINE OR MILK	250 ML

RUB THE INSIDE OF A 4-QUART SLOW COOKER BOWL WITH THE CUT CLOVE OF GARLIC, THEN DISCARD GARLIC. ADD CHEESE, FLOUR AND MUSTARD (IF USING), TOSSING TO COAT. POUR BEER OVER TOP. COVER AND COOK ON LOW FOR 3 TO 4 HOURS, STIRRING ONCE OR TWICE, UNTIL MELTED AND BUBBLING AROUND THE EDGES.

SERVES 8 OR MORE.

TIP: ANY OF YOUR FAVORITE MELTABLE CHEESES CAN BE USED IN PLACE OF THE GRUYÈRE AND/OR EMMENTAL.

TIP: SINCE YOU'RE USING A SLOW COOKER RATHER THAN A TRADITIONAL FONDUE POT, YOU CAN USE BAMBOO SKEWERS FOR DIPPING.

FRENCH ONION DIP

THE ONIONS ARE WHAT WE'RE SLOW COOKING HERE. DO IT THIS WAY ONCE AND YOU'LL NEVER REACH FOR A PACKET OF ONION SOUP MIX AGAIN! SERVE WITH SLICED BAGUETTE, CRACKERS OR RAW VEGETABLES.

2	LARGE ONIONS, CHOPPED	2
1	BAY LEAF (OPTIONAL)	1
1 TBSP	SUGAR	15 ML
2 TBSP	VEGETABLE OIL	30 ML
1 TSP	BUTTER, MELTED	5 ML
2 CUPS	SOUR CREAM	500 ML
1 CUP	MAYONNAISE	250 ML
PINCH	CAYENNE PEPPER	PINCH
	SALT TO TASTE	

COMBINE ONIONS, BAY LEAF (IF USING), SUGAR, OIL AND BUTTER IN A 4-QUART SLOW COOKER. COVER AND COOK ON LOW FOR 8 HOURS OR UNTIL ONIONS ARE SOFT AND GOLDEN. REMOVE FROM SLOW COOKER AND LET COOL. DISCARD BAY LEAF. IN A MEDIUM BOWL, COMBINE SOUR CREAM, MAYONNAISE AND CAYENNE. STIR IN ONIONS AND SEASON WITH SALT. MAKES ABOUT 4 CUPS (1 L).

ROASTED RED PEPPER AND FETA DIP

PEPPERS CAN BE COOKED THIS WAY FOR A NUMBER OF DISHES, BUT WE LIKE PURÉEING THEM WITH SALTY FETA FOR A TASTY DIP. SERVE WITH CUT-UP VEGGIES AND PITA CHIPS.

I TBSP	VEGETABLE OIL	15 ML
2	RED BELL PEPPERS, HALVED AND SEEDED	2
I	GARLIC CLOVE, MINCED	I
1 1/2 CUPS	CRUMBLED FETA CHEESE	375 ML
2 TBSP	CHOPPED FRESH CILANTRO	30 ML
1/2 TSP	GROUND CUMIN	2 ML
PINCH	SUGAR	PINCH
PINCH	CAYENNE PEPPER	PINCH
2 TBSP	LIME JUICE	30 ML
2 TSP	RED WINE VINEGAR	10 ML

RUB THE BOWL OF A 4-QUART SLOW COOKER WITH OIL AND PLACE PEPPERS INSIDE. COVER AND COOK ON LOW FOR 3 HOURS OR UNTIL PEPPERS ARE SOFT, WITH WRINKLY SKIN. LET STAND UNTIL COOL ENOUGH TO HANDLE, THEN PEEL OFF THE SKINS WITH YOUR FINGERS. IN A FOOD PROCESSOR, COMBINE PEELED PEPPERS, GARLIC, FETA, CILANTRO, CUMIN, SUGAR, CAYENNE, LIME JUICE AND VINEGAR; PROCESS UNTIL SMOOTH. TASTE AND ADJUST SEASONING. MAKES ABOUT 2 CUPS (500 ML).

TIP: COOKED PEPPERS CAN BE MADE AHEAD AND STORED IN THE FREEZER (THAW BEFORE USING FOR THIS DIP) OR IN THE FRIDGE, SUBMERGED IN OLIVE OIL, FOR UP TO 2 WEEKS.

BUFFALO BEAN DIP

THIS CHEESY VEGETARIAN DIP HAS THE SPICE AND ZING OF CLASSIC BUFFALO WINGS. SERVE WITH TORTILLA CHIPS.

1	PACKAGE (8 OZ/250 G) CREAM CHEESE, CUT INTO CUBES	1
1	CAN (19 OZ/540 ML) WHITE KIDNEY OR NAVY BEANS, RINSED AND DRAINED (2 CUPS/500 ML)	1
1/2 CUP	SHREDDED MOZZARELLA CHEESE	125 ML
1/2 CUP	BUFFALO-STYLE HOT PEPPER SAUCE (SUCH AS FRANK'S REDHOT)	125 ML
1/2 CUP	BLUE CHEESE DRESSING	125 ML

COMBINE ALL INGREDIENTS IN A 4-QUART SLOW COOKER, STIRRING TO DISTRIBUTE CREAM CHEESE EVENLY. COVER AND COOK ON LOW FOR 4 HOURS OR UNTIL CHEESE IS MELTED AND DIP IS HOT AND BUBBLING. STIR BEFORE SERVING. SERVES 6 TO 8.

"I'M TIRED OF ACQUIRING KNOWLEDGE. SOMEONE BRING ME A DRINK AND A WHOOPEE CUSHION."
– CORNELIUS TALBOT

CHILI CON QUESO DIP

PROCESSED CHEESE IS UNBEATABLE FOR ITS
MELTABILITY IN A CREAMY CLASSIC CON QUESO DIP.
SERVE WITH TORTILLA CHIPS FOR SCOOPING.

	VEGETABLE OIL	
2	FRESH CHORIZO OR ITALIAN SAUSAGES	2
1	SMALL ONION, FINELY CHOPPED	1
1	JALAPEÑO PEPPER, SEEDED AND FINELY CHOPPED (OPTIONAL)	1
2 TBSP	CHILI POWDER	30 ML
1 LB	PASTEURIZED PROCESSED CHEESE LOAF (SUCH AS VELVEETA), CUBED	500 G
1 CUP	SALSA	250 ML

IN A LARGE, HEAVY SKILLET, HEAT A DRIZZLE OF OIL
OVER MEDIUM-HIGH HEAT. SQUEEZE SAUSAGES OUT OF
THEIR CASINGS INTO THE PAN. ADD ONION AND JALAPEÑO
(IF USING); COOK, BREAKING THE MEAT UP WITH A SPOON,
UNTIL BROWNED AND NO LONGER PINK. STIR IN CHILI
POWDER. TRANSFER TO A 4-QUART SLOW COOKER AND
STIR IN CHEESE AND SALSA. COVER AND COOK ON LOW
FOR 2 TO 4 HOURS, STIRRING ONCE OR TWICE, UNTIL
MELTED AND BUBBLING AROUND THE EDGES. SERVE WARM.
SERVES 6 TO 8.

VARIATION: REPLACE THE SAUSAGES WITH 8 OZ (250 G)
GROUND BEEF.

CRAB AND ARTICHOKE DIP

SERVE THIS DIP RIGHT OUT OF A SMALL SLOW COOKER TO KEEP IT WARM ALL PARTY LONG. SERVE WITH SLICED BAGUETTE OR TORTILLA CHIPS.

4	GREEN ONIONS, CHOPPED	4
1	CAN (14 OZ/398 ML) ARTICHOKES, DRAINED AND CHOPPED	1
1	PACKAGE (8 OZ/250 G) CREAM CHEESE, CUBED	1
1	CAN (4 OZ/120 G) CRABMEAT, DRAINED	1
1/2 CUP	GRATED PARMESAN CHEESE	125 ML
1/2 TSP	DRY MUSTARD	2 ML
1/4 TSP	CAYENNE PEPPER	1 ML
2 TBSP	WORCESTERSHIRE SAUCE	30 ML
	JUICE OF 1 LEMON	

COMBINE ALL INGREDIENTS IN A 2- TO 4-QUART SLOW COOKER. COVER AND COOK ON LOW FOR 2 TO 3 HOURS OR UNTIL MELTED AND BUBBLING. SERVE WARM.

SERVES 6 TO 8.

BUFFALO CHICKEN DIP

THIS GOOEY, CHEESY DIP IS A GREAT WAY TO MAKE USE OF YOUR ROASTED CHICKEN OR TURKEY LEFTOVERS! IT STAYS WARM WHEN YOU SERVE IT STRAIGHT FROM THE SLOW COOKER. DON'T WORRY ABOUT MAKING A BIG BATCH — IT WILL GO FAST. (AND LEFTOVERS REHEAT BEAUTIFULLY, IF THERE ARE ANY.) SERVE WITH TORTILLA CHIPS, CRACKERS OR CARROT AND CELERY STICKS.

2	PACKAGES (EACH 8 OZ/250 G) CREAM CHEESE	2
2 CUPS	CHOPPED OR SHREDDED COOKED CHICKEN OR TURKEY	500 ML
1 CUP	SOUR CREAM	250 ML
3 CUPS	SHREDDED SHARP (OLD) WHITE OR ORANGE CHEDDAR OR GOUDA	750 ML
3/4 CUP	BUFFALO-STYLE HOT PEPPER SAUCE (SUCH AS FRANK'S REDHOT)	175 ML
1 CUP	SHREDDED MOZZARELLA CHEESE	250 ML
2 to 3	GREEN ONIONS, CHOPPED (OPTIONAL)	2 to 3

DROP CREAM CHEESE IN BLOBS OVER THE BOTTOM OF A 4- TO 6-QUART SLOW COOKER. TOP WITH CHICKEN, SOUR CREAM, CHEDDAR AND HOT SAUCE. COVER AND COOK ON LOW FOR 2 TO 4 HOURS OR UNTIL HEATED THROUGH AND BUBBLING. STIR AND TOP WITH MOZZARELLA AND GREEN ONIONS TO TASTE. COVER AND COOK FOR 10 MINUTES OR UNTIL MOZZARELLA HAS MELTED. SERVE WARM.

SERVES 8 TO 10.

TIP: IN PLACE OF THE GREEN ONIONS, YOU COULD USE 1/4 CUP (60 ML) CHOPPED FRESH CHIVES.

BUFFALO WINGS

YOU'LL NEVER LOOK AT WINGS IN THE PUB THE SAME WAY — THESE REALLY DO HAVE ONLY THREE INGREDIENTS! SERVE WITH CARROT AND CELERY STICKS, AND BLUE CHEESE DRESSING FOR DIPPING.

3 LBS	CHICKEN WINGS, SPLIT	1.5 KG
1 1/4 CUPS	BUFFALO-STYLE HOT PEPPER SAUCE (SUCH AS FRANK'S REDHOT), DIVIDED	300 ML
1/2 CUP	BUTTER	125 ML

COMBINE WINGS AND 1/2 CUP (125 ML) HOT SAUCE IN A 4- TO 6-QUART SLOW COOKER. COVER AND COOK ON LOW FOR 3 1/2 TO 4 1/2 HOURS OR UNTIL WINGS ARE COOKED THROUGH BUT NOT ACTUALLY FALLING OFF THE BONE.

MEANWHILE, IN A SMALL SAUCEPAN, HEAT BUTTER AND THE REMAINING HOT SAUCE OVER MEDIUM HEAT UNTIL COMBINED (OR USE THE MICROWAVE). TRANSFER HALF TO A BOWL FOR SERVING AND SET THE OTHER HALF ASIDE.

PREHEAT THE BROILER AND SET A RACK 6 INCHES (15 CM) BELOW IT. LINE A LARGE RIMMED BAKING SHEET WITH FOIL AND SPRAY THE FOIL WITH NONSTICK COOKING SPRAY. TRANSFER WINGS TO THE FOIL AND ARRANGE IN A SINGLE LAYER. BROIL FOR 1 TO 2 MINUTES ON EACH SIDE, TURNING ONCE, UNTIL CRISPED TO YOUR LIKING. POUR THE RESERVED HOT SAUCE MIXTURE OVER THE WINGS AND TOSS TO COAT. BROIL FOR ANOTHER 1 TO 2 MINUTES, WATCHING CAREFULLY, UNTIL WINGS AND SAUCE ARE SIZZLING. TRANSFER TO A SERVING PLATTER AND SERVE WITH THE EXTRA HOT SAUCE MIXTURE. SERVES 8 OR MORE.

BARBECUE WINGS

YOU CAN USE BOTTLED BARBECUE SAUCE FOR THESE IF YOU WISH, OR TRY OUR RHUBARB OR SASKATOON BERRY VERSIONS (PAGES 261 OR 262).

1 TBSP	PACKED BROWN SUGAR	15 ML
1 TBSP	CHILI POWDER	15 ML
1/4 TSP	BLACK PEPPER	1 ML
	SALT TO TASTE	
1 TBSP	VEGETABLE OIL	15 ML
3 LBS	CHICKEN WINGS, SPLIT	1.5 KG
3/4 CUP	BARBECUE SAUCE	175 ML

IN A SMALL BOWL, COMBINE BROWN SUGAR, CHILI POWDER, PEPPER, SALT AND OIL. TOSS WINGS AND THE BROWN SUGAR MIXTURE TOGETHER IN A 4- TO 6-QUART SLOW COOKER. COVER AND COOK ON LOW FOR $3\frac{1}{2}$ TO $4\frac{1}{2}$ HOURS OR UNTIL WINGS ARE COOKED THROUGH BUT NOT ACTUALLY FALLING OFF THE BONE.

PREHEAT THE BROILER AND SET A RACK 6 INCHES (15 CM) BELOW IT. LINE A LARGE RIMMED BAKING SHEET WITH FOIL AND SPRAY THE FOIL WITH NONSTICK COOKING SPRAY. TRANSFER WINGS TO THE FOIL AND ARRANGE IN A SINGLE LAYER. BROIL FOR 1 TO 2 MINUTES ON EACH SIDE, TURNING ONCE, UNTIL CRISPED TO YOUR LIKING. POUR BARBECUE SAUCE OVER THE WINGS AND TOSS TO COAT. BROIL FOR ANOTHER 1 TO 2 MINUTES, WATCHING CAREFULLY, UNTIL WINGS AND SAUCE ARE SIZZLING. TRANSFER TO A SERVING PLATTER. *SERVES 8 OR MORE.*

SWEET-AND-SPICY WINGS

THESE ARE EXACTLY WHAT THEY SAY THEY ARE — HAVE NAPKINS AND FINGER BOWLS ON HAND!

2	GARLIC CLOVES, MINCED	2
3/4 CUP	SUGAR	175 ML
2 TBSP	FISH SAUCE	30 ML
2 TBSP	SRIRACHA	30 ML
3 LBS	CHICKEN WINGS, SPLIT	1.5 KG
1/2 TSP	CORNSTARCH	2 ML
2 TSP	WATER	10 ML
	CHOPPED FRESH BASIL, CILANTRO OR MINT (OPTIONAL)	

COMBINE GARLIC, SUGAR, FISH SAUCE AND SRIRACHA IN A 4- TO 6-QUART SLOW COOKER. ADD WINGS AND TOSS TO COAT. COVER AND COOK ON LOW FOR 3 TO 4 HOURS OR UNTIL WINGS ARE COOKED THROUGH BUT NOT ACTUALLY FALLING OFF THE BONE.

IN A SMALL SAUCEPAN, COMBINE CORNSTARCH AND WATER. LADLE 1 CUP (250 ML) LIQUID OUT OF THE SLOW COOKER AND INTO THE PAN. WHISK, THEN BRING TO A BOIL OVER HIGH HEAT. REDUCE HEAT AND SIMMER FOR AT LEAST 1 MINUTE OR UNTIL THICKENED (WATCH CAREFULLY, AS IT BOILS UP QUICKLY).

PREHEAT THE BROILER AND SET A RACK 8 INCHES (20 CM) BELOW IT. LINE A LARGE RIMMED BAKING SHEET WITH FOIL AND SPRAY THE FOIL WITH NONSTICK COOKING SPRAY. TRANSFER WINGS TO THE FOIL AND ARRANGE IN A SINGLE LAYER. BROIL FOR 2 TO 3 MINUTES ON EACH SIDE, TURNING ONCE, UNTIL CRISPED TO YOUR LIKING. POUR

THE THICKENED SAUCE OVER THE WINGS AND TOSS TO
COAT. BROIL FOR ANOTHER 1 TO 2 MINUTES, WATCHING
CAREFULLY, UNTIL WINGS AND SAUCE ARE SIZZLING.
TRANSFER TO A SERVING PLATTER AND SPRINKLE WITH
BASIL (IF USING). SERVES 8 OR MORE.

VARIATION

HONEY GARLIC WINGS: INCREASE THE GARLIC TO 5 OR
6 CLOVES, REPLACE THE SUGAR WITH AN EQUAL AMOUNT
OF LIQUID HONEY, REPLACE THE FISH SAUCE WITH
$1\frac{1}{2}$ TBSP (22 ML) SOY SAUCE, OMIT THE SRIRACHA AND
ADD $\frac{1}{4}$ TSP (1 ML) SALT TO THE SAUCE. SERVE SPRINKLED
WITH CHOPPED GREEN ONIONS AND SESAME SEEDS IN
PLACE OF THE FRESH HERBS.

I'M STARTING TO THINK I'LL NEVER BE
OLD ENOUGH TO KNOW BETTER.

HOISIN PORK MEATBALLS

PERFECT FOR PARTIES!

1/4 CUP	DRY BREAD CRUMBS	60 ML
1	EGG, LIGHTLY BEATEN	1
1 LB	GROUND PORK	500 G
3	GREEN ONIONS, CHOPPED	3
1/2 TSP	SALT	2 ML
1/4 TSP	BLACK PEPPER	1 ML
	VEGETABLE OIL	
2	GARLIC CLOVES, MINCED	2
1 TBSP	GRATED FRESH GINGER	15 ML
1/4 CUP	HOISIN SAUCE	60 ML
2 TBSP	RICE VINEGAR	30 ML
1 TBSP	SOY SAUCE	15 ML

IN A LARGE BOWL, COMBINE BREAD CRUMBS AND EGG. LET STAND FOR A FEW MINUTES SO THE CRUMBS ABSORB SOME MOISTURE FROM THE EGG. USING YOUR HANDS, MIX IN PORK, GREEN ONIONS, SALT AND PEPPER UNTIL JUST COMBINED. SHAPE INTO 30 SMALL MEATBALLS.

IN A LARGE SKILLET, HEAT A DRIZZLE OF OIL OVER MEDIUM-HIGH HEAT. WORKING IN BATCHES, BROWN MEATBALLS ON ALL SIDES — THEY DON'T HAVE TO BE COOKED THROUGH. TRANSFER TO A 4- TO 6-QUART SLOW COOKER AS YOU GO. IN A SMALL BOWL, COMBINE GARLIC, GINGER, HOISIN SAUCE, VINEGAR AND SOY SAUCE. POUR OVER MEATBALLS AND GENTLY TOSS TO COAT. COVER AND COOK ON LOW FOR 4 TO 6 HOURS OR UNTIL MEATBALLS ARE NO LONGER PINK INSIDE. SERVE WARM. MAKES 30 MEATBALLS.

BUFFALO CHICKEN MEATBALLS

THE TASTE OF BUFFALO WINGS — WITHOUT THE BONES. TO STREAMLINE THINGS, PICK UP A PACKAGE OF FROZEN CHICKEN MEATBALLS. SERVE WITH BLUE CHEESE DRESSING FOR DIPPING.

3/4 CUP	BUFFALO-STYLE HOT PEPPER SAUCE (SUCH AS FRANK'S REDHOT)	175 ML
1/2 CUP	BUTTER	125 ML
2 TBSP	WHITE VINEGAR	30 ML
2 LBS	GROUND CHICKEN OR TURKEY	1 KG
1 CUP	FRESH BREAD CRUMBS	250 ML
1	GREEN ONION, FINELY CHOPPED	1
1	LARGE EGG	1
	SALT AND BLACK PEPPER TO TASTE	

COMBINE HOT SAUCE, BUTTER AND VINEGAR IN A 4- TO 6-QUART SLOW COOKER. IN A LARGE BOWL, USING YOUR HANDS, COMBINE CHICKEN, BREAD CRUMBS, GREEN ONION, EGG, SALT AND PEPPER. SHAPE INTO 1-INCH (2.5 CM) BALLS AND NESTLE IN THE HOT SAUCE, GENTLY TURNING TO COAT. COVER AND COOK ON LOW FOR 4 TO 6 HOURS OR UNTIL MEATBALLS ARE NO LONGER PINK INSIDE AND SAUCE IS THICKENED AND BUBBLING. SERVE WARM, WITH TOOTHPICKS AND NAPKINS ON HAND. SERVES 6.

OLD-SCHOOL JELLY MEATBALLS

WE'VE BEEN MAKING THESE COCKTAIL MEATBALLS WITH GRAPE JELLY FOR AS LONG AS WE'VE BEEN HAVING PARTIES. IT DOESN'T GET MUCH EASIER, AND THEY'RE EVERYONE'S FAVORITE.

1	BAG (2 LBS/1 KG) FULLY COOKED FROZEN MEATBALLS	1
1 CUP	KETCHUP OR CHILI SAUCE (OR A COMBINATION)	250 ML
1 CUP	GRAPE JELLY	250 ML
2 TBSP	LEMON JUICE	30 ML

COMBINE ALL INGREDIENTS IN A 4- TO 6-QUART SLOW COOKER. COVER AND COOK ON LOW FOR 3 TO 4 HOURS, STIRRING ONCE OR TWICE, UNTIL HEATED THROUGH AND BUBBLING AROUND THE EDGES. SERVE WARM, WITH TOOTHPICKS AND NAPKINS ON HAND. SERVES 8 TO 10.

EVENING NEWS IS WHEN THEY BEGIN WITH "GOOD EVENING" AND USE THE NEXT HOUR TO TELL YOU WHY IT ISN'T.

HONEY GARLIC MEATBALLS

SOMETIMES, A BAG OF FROZEN MEATBALLS IS JUST THE THING. THESE SWEET AND TANGY MEATBALLS HIT ALL THE RIGHT NOTES AND ARE ALWAYS AMONG THE FIRST TO GO AT PARTIES.

1	BAG (2 LBS/1 KG) FULLY COOKED FROZEN MEATBALLS	1
1/2 CUP	KETCHUP	125 ML
1/3 CUP	LIQUID HONEY	75 ML
1/4 CUP	PACKED BROWN SUGAR	60 ML
2 TBSP	SOY SAUCE	30 ML
2	GARLIC CLOVES, MINCED	2

COMBINE ALL INGREDIENTS IN A 4- TO 6-QUART SLOW COOKER. COVER AND COOK ON LOW FOR 3 TO 4 HOURS, STIRRING OCCASIONALLY, UNTIL HEATED THROUGH AND BUBBLING AROUND THE EDGES. SERVE WARM, WITH TOOTHPICKS AND NAPKINS ON HAND. SERVES 8 TO 10.

HOISIN CHICKEN LETTUCE WRAPS

LETTUCE WRAPS ARE FUN FOR A PARTY. LET GUESTS LOAD A LETTUCE LEAF WITH FILLING, WRAP AND EAT. WE LIKE SERVING THESE ON GAME NIGHT — IT'S A MUNCHABLE SORT OF DINNER YOU CAN EAT ON THE COUCH.

6	BONELESS SKINLESS CHICKEN THIGHS	6
2 to 3	GREEN ONIONS, CHOPPED	2 to 3
1	SMALL RED BELL PEPPER, CHOPPED	1
1	GARLIC CLOVE, CRUSHED	1
2 TSP	GRATED FRESH GINGER	10 ML
1/2 CUP	HOISIN SAUCE	125 ML
	BUTTER OR LEAF LETTUCE LEAVES	

COMBINE CHICKEN, GREEN ONIONS, RED PEPPER, GARLIC, GINGER AND HOISIN SAUCE IN THE BOWL OF A 4- TO 6-QUART SLOW COOKER. COVER AND COOK ON LOW FOR 4 TO 6 HOURS OR UNTIL CHICKEN IS VERY TENDER. SHRED THE CHICKEN WITH TWO FORKS. SERVE IN A BOWL, WITH LETTUCE LEAVES ALONGSIDE TO FILL, WRAP AND EAT. SERVES 4 TO 6.

VARIATION

BUFFALO CHICKEN LETTUCE WRAPS: DITCH THE GINGER AND SWAP 1/2 CUP (125 ML) BUFFALO-STYLE HOT PEPPER SAUCE (SUCH AS FRANK'S REDHOT) AND 1/4 CUP (60 ML) BUTTER FOR THE HOISIN SAUCE.